Bernie Smithwick and THE PURPLE SHOESTRING

William Coleman
Illustrated by Joan Artley Sterner

from David C. Cook Publishing Co.

I LOVE TO READ BOOKS encourage children to read—all by themselves. Each Bible-based reader uses simple vocabulary repeated over and over. Its lilting rhythm will inspire your child to exclaim, "I love to read!" Soon the child will read another book and another and another. Before you know it, this love of books will last a lifetime!

Early Readers in the I LOVE TO READ SERIES:
In the Land of the Music Machine
Return to the Land of the Music Machine
In, Out, and About Catfish Pond
Up, Down, and Around the Raintree
Abram, Abram, Where Are We Going?
Look What You've Done Now, Moses
Bernie Smithwick and the Super Red Ball
Bernie Smithwick and the Purple Shoestring

Chariot Books is an imprint of David C. Cook Publishing Co.

David C. Cook Publishing Co., Elgin, Illinois 60120
David C. Cook Publishing Co., Weston, Ontario

BERNIE SMITHWICK AND THE PURPLE SHOESTRING

Cover and illustrations by Joan Artley Sterner

First Printing, 1984
Printed in the United States of America

89 88 87 86 85 84 5 4 3 2

Library of Congress Cataloging in Publication Data

Coleman, William.
Bernie Smithwick and the purple shoestring.
(I love to read)
Summary: Bernie must take the consequences when he loses his temper.
1. Children's stories, American. [1. Anger—Fiction] I. Sterner, Joan Artley, ill. II. Title.
PZ7.C67725Be 1984 [E] 84-12138
ISBN 0-89191-824-8 (pbk.)

For Kellen Peterson

Bernie Smithwick woke up
early on Tuesday morning.
Tuesday was going to be a
special day for Bernie.

All the children
in his class
planned to wear
something new.

Bernie thought and thought
about what to wear.

First Bernie put on
an eye patch
like pirates wear.

But the eye patch
kept slipping down
over his nose.

Then Bernie put on
a straw hat
like some farmers wear.

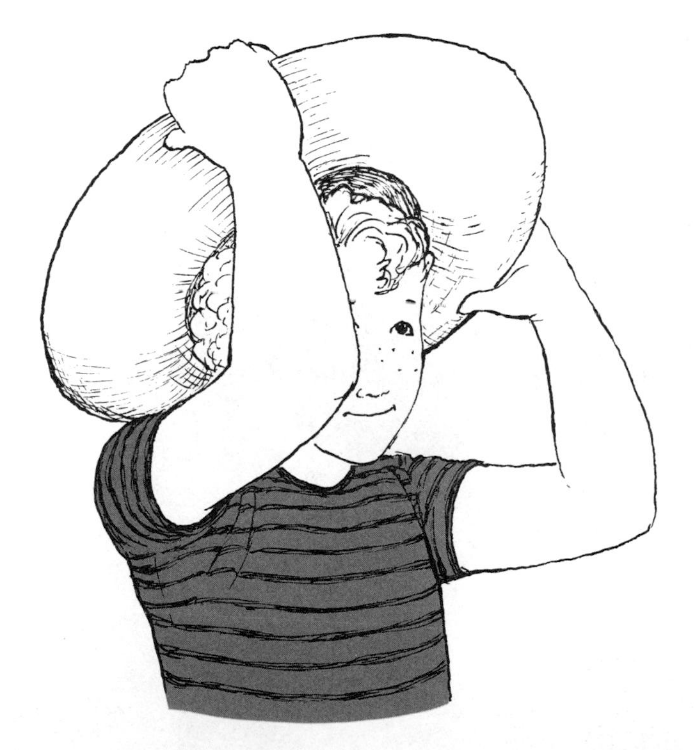

But the straw hat
was too big.
It covered Bernie's
eyes and ears.

Next Bernie put on
a big pair of
yellow sun glasses.

Roscoe the cat
made a funny face
at the sun glasses.

Finally Bernie found
just the right
thing to wear.

He picked up
a pair of
purple shoestrings.

His Aunt Ann
had given them to Bernie.
But Bernie had
never worn them.

Great!

Bernie thought
as he held the
purple shoestrings high.
These are just right!

But Roscoe the cat
made another
funny face.

Bernie took the
old strings out of
his shoes.
He began putting a
purple shoestring
in one shoe.

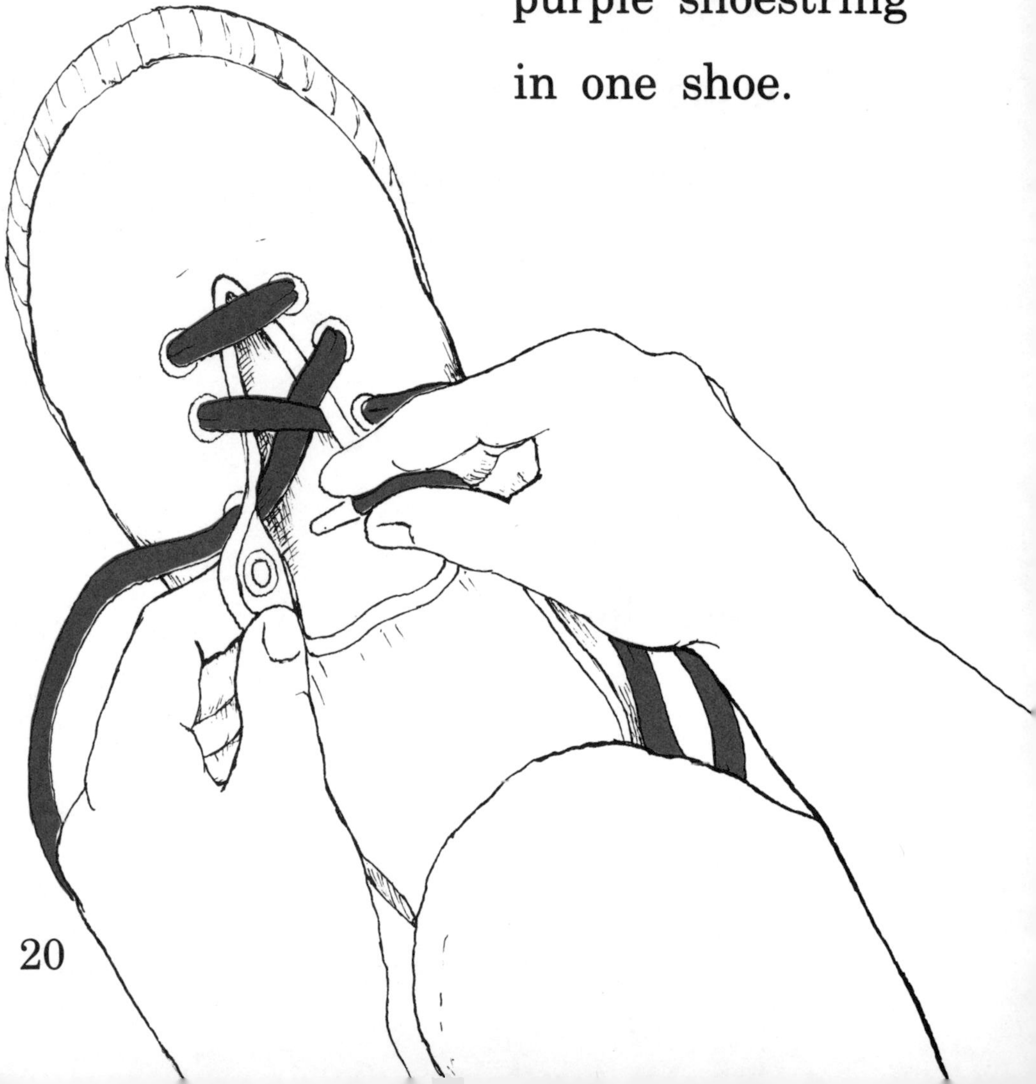

Bernie looked at
the clock.
It was getting late.
He would have to hurry
to be at school
on time.

"There,"
Bernie said to himself.
"I've got the first
shoestring in."

Bernie looked for the
second purple shoestring.

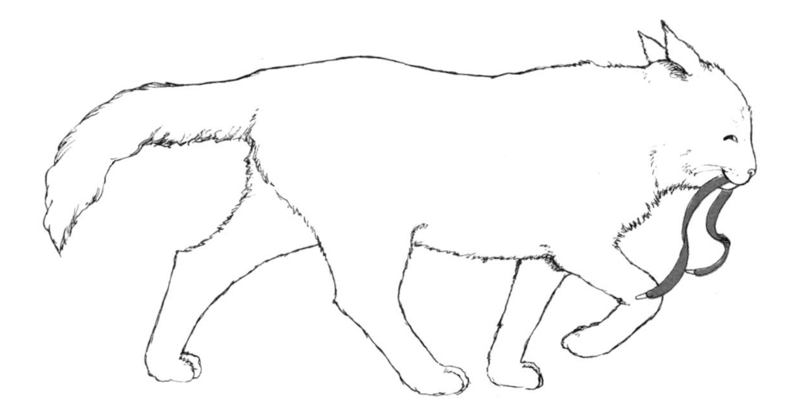

"Where is it?"
he asked.
Bernie had put
the shoestring
on the bed.
At least,
he thought he had.
But the purple shoestring
wasn't on the bed.

Bernie looked
under the bed.
No purple shoestring.
Bernie looked
beside the bed.
No purple shoestring.
Bernie looked
around the bed.
Still no purple shoestring.

Then Bernie saw
Roscoe the cat
sitting on a chair.
Roscoe had a big smile
on his face and
a purple shoestring
in his mouth.

"Be a good cat,"
said Bernie.
He stepped toward Roscoe.
"Give Bernie the
purple shoestring."

Bernie held out
his hand for
the purple shoestring.
Roscoe jumped away.

With a smile on his face
and a purple shoestring
in his mouth,
Roscoe ran
behind the door.

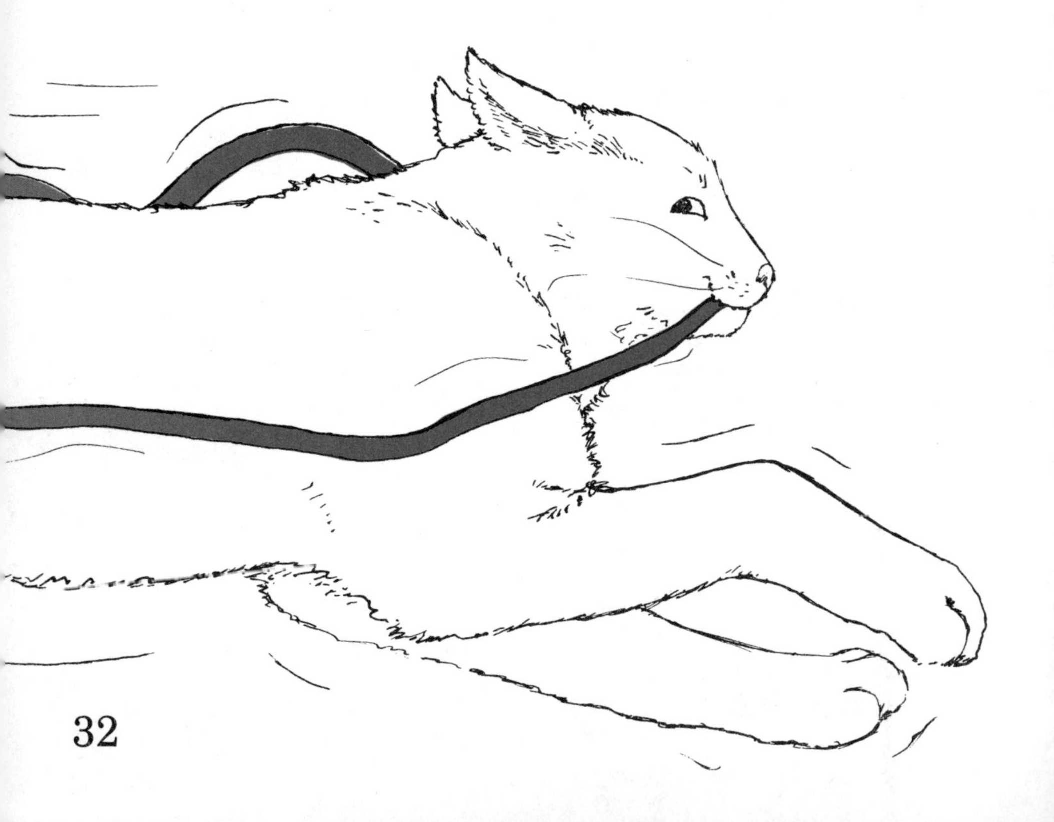

"Roscoe, don't make me
late for school,"
Bernie said as he
walked toward the cat.

Roscoe ran into
the living room
and hid under
the couch.
And Roscoe smiled
with the purple shoestring
in his mouth.

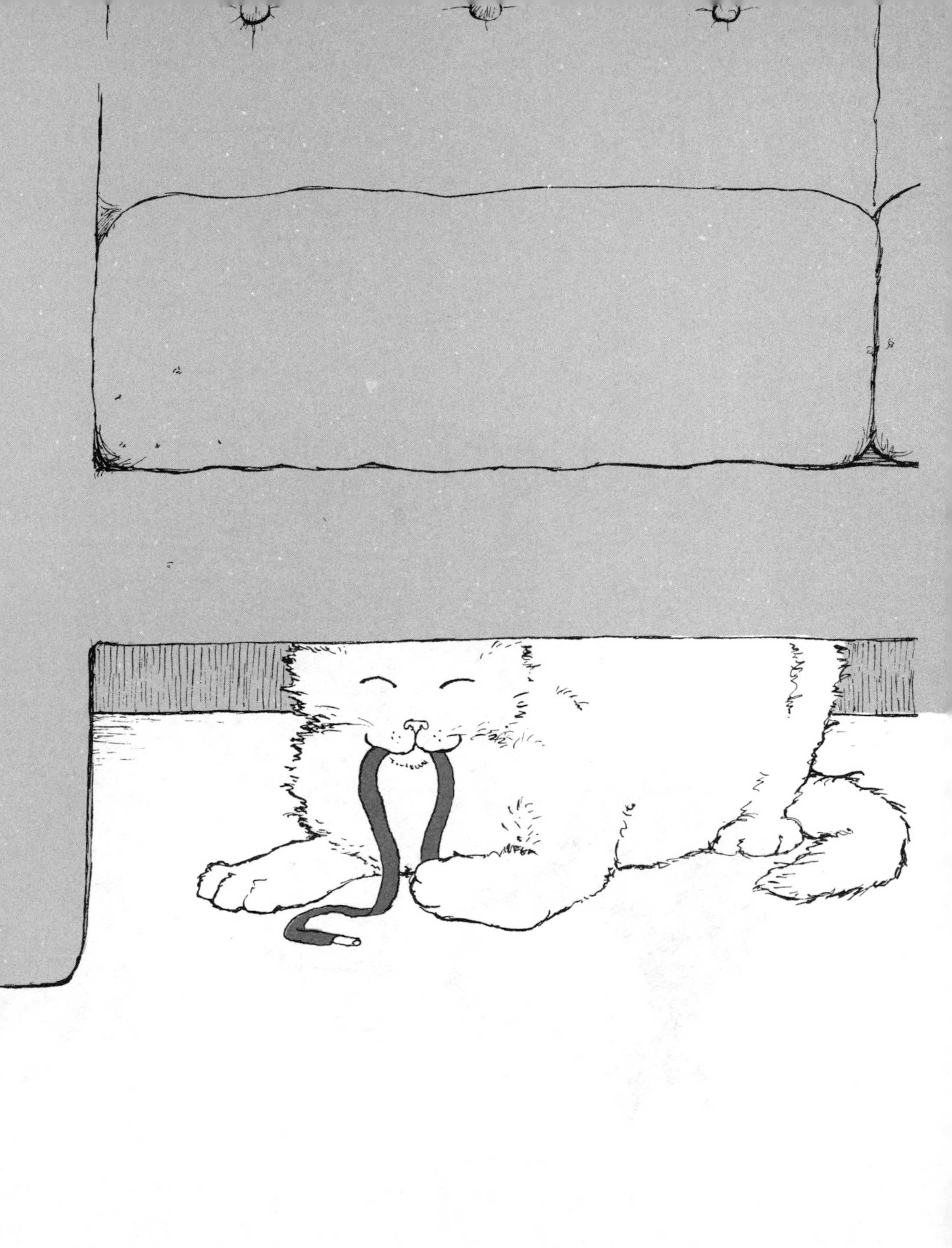

Bernie yelled at Roscoe,
"Give me my shoestring!"
Bernie reached
under the couch
to get Roscoe the cat.
But he couldn't reach Roscoe.

Bernie was becoming angry.
He threw a ball
under the couch.
Then Bernie threw his shoe
under the couch.

Roscoe ran behind
the tall lamp.
Bernie tried to grab him
and knocked the lamp over.

Roscoe ran into the kitchen
and sat under the table.
Bernie ran after him.

Bernie's face was red.
"I'll get you!"
Bernie yelled as
he opened the
refrigerator door.

Bernie took out a can
of whipped cream and
began to shake it.
Roscoe's eyes were big.
He looked at Bernie.

Bernie sprayed
the whipped cream
at Roscoe the cat.
The cream hit the floor.
It missed Roscoe the cat.

Roscoe quickly
jumped on a chair.
He smiled with the purple
shoestring in his mouth.

Bernie sprayed more cream
at Roscoe.
Whipped cream went
all over the wall.

As Roscoe ran out
of the kitchen,
Bernie sprayed
whipped cream
all over the floor.

Just then Bernie's mother
came into the kitchen.
She saw whipped cream
all over the wall
and all over the floor.

"Oh, no!"

Bernie's mother screamed.

(Sometimes mothers do that.)

"You will clean up
every drop of cream,"
said Bernie's mother.

"But I needed my
purple shoestring."
Bernie picked up
the shoestring that Roscoe
had dropped in the cream
as he ran out of the kitchen.

And Roscoe the cat smiled.

Bernie cleaned up the cream.
He found his shoe
under the couch.
He put the purple shoestring
in his shoe.
Bernie was very late
for school
on Tuesday morning.

"A quick-tempered man does foolish things."

Proverbs 14:17, NIV

Vocabulary

Of the 210 words used in this book, 190 are recommended by the Ginn Lexicon for grades one and two. The words recommended for grade three and above are starred.

a
about
after
all
an
and
angry
Ann*
another
are
around
as
asked
at
Aunt
away

ball
be
becoming
bed
began
behind
Bernie*
beside
big
but

came
can
cat
chair
children
class
clean
cleaned
clock
couch*
couldn't
covered
cream

day
do
does
don't
door
down
drop
dropped

early
ears
every
eye
eyes

face
farmers
finally
first
floor
foolish*
for
found
funny

get
getting
give
given
glasses
going
good
got
grab
great

had
hand
hat
have
he
held
hid*
high
him
himself
his
hit
hurry

I
I'll
in
into
is
it
I've*

jumped
just

kept
kitchen
knocked

lamp*
late
least
like
living
looked

made
make
man
me
missed
more
morning
mother
mouth
my

needed
never
new
next
no
nose

of
oh
old
on
one
opened
out
over

pair
patch*
picked
pirates*
planned
Proverbs*
purple*
put
putting

quickly
quick-tempered*

ran
reach
reached
red
refrigerator*
right
room
Roscoe*

said
sat
saw
school
screamed
second
shake
shoe
shoes
shoestrings*
sitting
slipping
smile
smiled
Smithwick*
some
something
sometimes
special
sprayed*
stopped
still
straw
strings
sun

table
tall
that
the
them
then
there
these
thing
things
thought
threw
time
to
too
took
toward
tried*
Tuesday*

under
up

very

walked
wall
was
wasn't
wear
went
were
what
where
whipped*
will
with
woke
worn*
would

yelled
yellow
you